Sailing is Fun!

A Beginners Manual for Young Sailors

By Charles D. Dawson

While sailing is potentially wonderful fun, it can also present significant dangers to the safety and lives of children and adults alike. Although efforts have been made to point out some of the more obvious dangers, it is well beyond the scope of this volume to identify all sources of possible danger associated with this pursuit in all places and under all circumstances and conditions. A safe and rewarding sailing experience ultimately depends on a clear-headed and well-informed adult understanding of the risks associated with each sailing situation. The exercise of sound judgment while inspecting sailing craft, in setting rules for use of the boat, in carefully applying an appropriate level of supervision, and imposing other appropriate controls on young sailors is vital.

First printing 2008

DEDICATION

Not long ago, I was thinking about teaching my grandson, Caleb, how to sail. I looked in book stores and on-line for a simple, kid-oriented instruction manual that he could use for study and reference, but I could not find anything suitable.

When I told Caleb about my problem, he said "Well, Grandpa, you know how to sail, why don't you write the book yourself."

Caleb planted the seed, and the rest, as they say, is history.

This book is dedicated to my grandchildren Caleb Brooks Dawson, and his sister, Logan Grace Dawson. Logan will be the next student at Grandpa Dawson's Stony Lake Sailing School.

THANKS

This volume would never have made its way to its present marketable form without the strong encouragement of my dear wife, Linda, who has also become one of my best editors.

Thanks, too, to my son John for his clever illustrations.

And finally, thanks to my old friend and sailing buddy, John P. Jack, for his advice and support. My "Dump Drill" sequence borrows heavily from a suggestion provided by Captain Jack.

FOREWARD

A Note to the Supervising Adult(s):

This book is written for children. My expectation was that a child should be educationally mature enough to read the book (perhaps with help), and be sufficiently physically developed to safely participate in sailing activity.

The original volume was produced for my grandson, Caleb, who was 5 at the time he read it, and he did well under instruction.

There are, of course, many kinds of sailboats. I find that 12-14 foot "board boats" are quite suitable for teaching children to sail, particularly on "flat water", and this is the type of boat I have used in my illustrations.

In my experience, most children, once properly introduced, come to enjoy sailing very much. There are those few, however, who simply have no interest. I advise patience. Try to introduce the subject a few times. If no interest is shown, put the matter off for a year or so. If, after repeated attempts you still get no response—well—it is simply not meant to be.

Initially, one must consider how the child feels around water, and what the child is capable of when *in* the water. Being fearful in or around water, while not so unusual, is not a particularly good way to begin sailing lessons. Patience and understanding are again the key.

There is a lot of water on this planet, and being able to swim and otherwise handle one's self comfortably in water are vitally important life skills. To this end, a child who cannot swim, or who is fearful or reticent around water should ultimately be referred to a water safety expert for advice, and perhaps instruction.

When the child is, hopefully, able to swim, and is otherwise comfortable around water, it's time to begin.

And when it's time to go out on the boat, we *begin* by putting on our life jackets. Everyone on the boat. Every time. No exceptions! Yes, I know, you are a good swimmer, but there are just too many thing that can go wrong. <u>Life jackets, please!</u>

Also remember to regularly inspect the sailboat you will be using. Old, cracked, decayed or deteriorated parts and fittings can be a safety hazard. They can also seriously "mess up" what might otherwise have been an enjoyable outing. Suppose that you are sailing along, a key part fails, and you have no way to control the boat. You will need to be "rescued". How will your young charge feel about the experience?

In order for a child to become a competent, confident and enthusiastic sailor, it is important to avoid, if at all possible, exposing the child to frightening experiences. These are not miniature "Rambos" we are dealing with here, and we should not expect them to be.

Initially, I highly recommend that the supervising adult act as "skipper" and that the young student serve as "crew".

During your first few sails, talk about the boat, the names for the various parts, and how they work. Demonstrate the points of sailing. Tack by coming about, and by jibing (if conditions will permit you to do that safely). Pinch up into irons and demonstrate how to get out of it. (Read this book first if you need to refresh).

When the child seems ready, go out sailing with the youngster at the tiller, and the adult as the crew.

Ultimately, most children will want to go out sailing alone. This, of course, should be permitted only when it is **safe**. In this regard, there are many things to consider. How competent is the youngster in the water? Are sailing skills and confidence adequately developed? What other boats will likely be on the water. (Power boat traffic tends to create large wakes which can make handling a 12-14 foot sail boat very difficult).

Are there areas in the watercourse in question which are deceptively shallow, or are known to hide submerged obstacles? What may be *in* the water? Inland lakes in Florida often harbor alligators. It is well beyond the scope of this book to point out all potential dangers and problems. I can recommend only that the matter be carefully and thoughtfully evaluated before permission is given.

Another thing to be considered is how an accidental capsize (tip-over) will be handled. With a younger, smaller child, continuous, close adult supervision is recommended, with a "chase boat" at the ready.

An older child with good aquatic skills may be subject to somewhat looser supervision, particularly if he or she is able to "right" the boat alone. It is generally thought that it takes a person weighing about 100 pounds and standing on the dagger board to right a boat of the size we are discussing. In this regard, I strongly recommend that before a solo sail is authorized, an adult-supervised "dump drill" should take place, where the process of righting the boat is practiced. See pages 21-22.

Next, set boundaries. "Stay close to our side of the lake, and don't sail past Green Point". It is highly advisable that young solo sailors be instructed to stay *within the supervising adult's field of vision* at all times, and that there be a working "chase boat" at hand in case of unexpected difficulties.

Table of Contents

Sailing is Fun!

Hi kids! This book is written just for you.

Sailing really is lots of fun. It's a great way to be outdoors, and to enjoy the sun, the wind and the water. And *guess what*! Sailing in your sailboat lets you go fast and have fun without polluting the environment!

So, let's get started. First, I suggest that you look this book over before you go sailing.

When you are just starting to learn about sailing, you need to go out with a grown-up who will be the **skipper** of the boat. (The skipper is the person who controls the boat).

See how the sail is raised. Watch what the skipper does. See how the skipper steers the boat and controls the sail. And always *ask lots of questions*. That's the best way to learn.

But when you are getting on the boat, <u>be sure that everyone on the boat is wearing a life jacket</u>. <u>Every time</u>. <u>No exceptions.</u> It's great to have fun, but it's really important to be safe, and no one can be safe on a boat without wearing a life jacket.

When you come back from your sail, help the skipper take the sail down and put the boat away. The more you learn about your boat, the better sailor you will be.

As soon as you have time, look over this book again. Your experiences on the water should help you to better understand what is written here.

Each time you go out, you will probably learn new things. Then one day, when the grown-up who is responsible for supervising you says that you are ready, and that the weather conditions are right, **you will likely get to try your hand at being the skipper!** The first few time you go out, you should have a grown-up on board, or at least close by with you in sight at all times and with a chase boat handy.

Here are some Sailing Words
you will want to know

The Skipper The Skipper is the person who controls the boat.

Batten, Batten Pocket Battens are stiff pieces of wood or plastic that fit into the batten pockets on the sail. Battens help the sail keep it's shape.

Sail The sail catches the wind and makes the boat go.

Boom The boom is the pole at the bottom of the sail. The boom is connected to the mast.

Rudder The rudder is used to steer the boat.

Tiller Bar The tiller bar is the handle on top of the rudder. The Skipper pushes or pulls on the tiller bar to steer the boat

Sheet Rope The sheet rope is connected to the boom. The Skipper uses the sheet rope to control the sail.

Dagger Board The dagger board is under water. It helps keep the boat from slipping sideways. The dagger board is pulled up and removed when the boat is coming in to shore.

Mainsail Halyard The mainsail halyard is the rope that is used to pull the sail up the mast.

Forestay & Side Stays The forestay and the side stays, (which are also called **shrouds**), are pieces of wire which secure the mast and keep it in place.

Mast The mast is the very tall pole to which the boom and sail are attached.

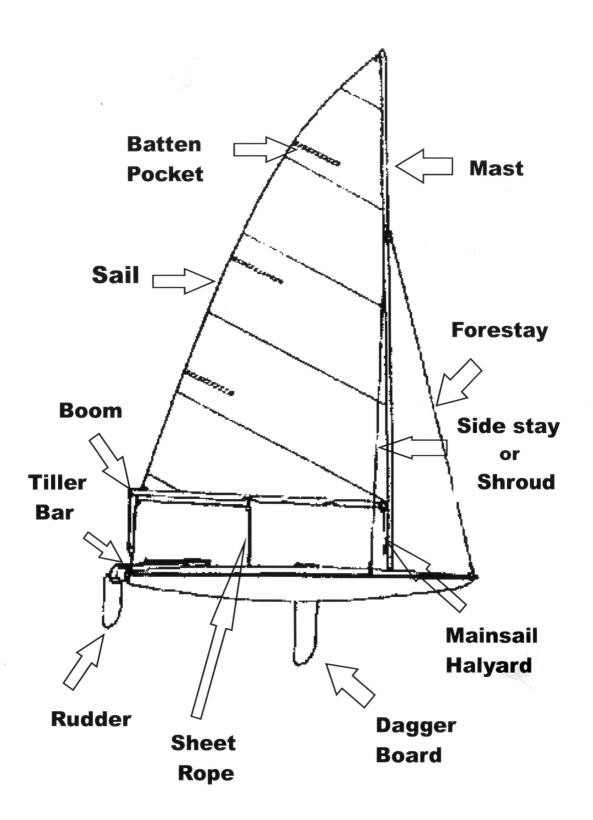

Batten Pocket

Mast

Sail

Forestay

Boom

Side stay or Shroud

Tiller Bar

Mainsail Halyard

Rudder

Sheet Rope

Dagger Board

More Sailing Words to know

The front of the boat is called the **"bow"**.
That word rhymes with **"wow"**.

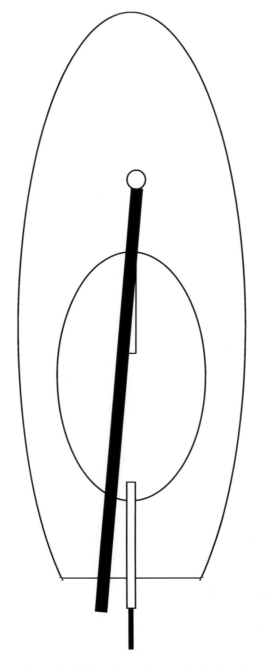

The left side
of the boat is
called the
"port"
side.

The right side
of the boat is
called the
"starboard"
side.

The back end of the boat is called the **"stern"**.

Safety First Always!

- Never go sailing without permission. Always be sure that a grown-up knows where you are, and is keeping an eye on you while you are sailing.

- Always wear a life jacket when sailing. Every time. No Exceptions.

- Never go sailing when there might be lightning.

- Never stand up on a small sailboat.

- Always keep an eye on the "boom". Remember that the boom will go from one side of the boat to the other when the skipper tacks (turns) the boat. Be careful that the "boom" does not hit you.

- The "Skipper" (the Captain), who is controlling the boat, always has the sheet rope in one hand, and the tiller bar in the other hand.

- Remember that the Skipper always sits on the "High Side" of the boat. That means the Skipper always has the wind at his or her back. If the Skipper were to sit on the "Low Side" facing the wind, the boat would be likely to tip over.

- If the sailboat does tip over, don't get excited. Hang on while the boat is tipping. When the sail touches the water, you slip into the water, and work your way around to the "bottom" of the boat which is now on it's side. Be careful not to get tangled in the sheet rope or the stays Do not **ever** try to swim under the boat or under the sail. If the grown-up who is supervising you has not gone through a "Dump Drill" with you, ask for one. Also check out page 21 of this book to learn what you have to do to get your boat upright.

The Wind!

The wind makes a sailboat go.

A Skipper must always know the "direction" of the wind. Where is the wind coming from? This can get *very tricky,* even for an experienced sailor!

When you are sailing on your boat and looking ahead to where the boat is going, you may feel "wind" in your face and think that the wind is coming toward you from straight ahead of the boat. But that is probably not right.

Do you remember a time when you were riding your bike really fast? Did it feel like there was a strong wind blowing in your face? But that was not real wind. It was what sailors call the "wind of motion". In other words, as you sail, you are moving through the air, and it *feels* like there is wind in your face, but that is not the real wind.

The problem with finding the direction of the wind is that the wind is invisible. But if you watch carefully, the wind will leave clues for you.

Look at the surface of the water. The wind will create little ripples which show it's direction. Also, look at flags and trees on the shore.

Many skippers will tie pieces of yarn on their forestay and their side stays. These are called "tell-tales" or "woolies" and can help tell wind direction.

It takes lots of practice to learn to tell the wind's true direction, but it is something a skipper has to figure out.

A Sailboat Cannot Sail
Directly Into the Wind

Let's say that you are sailing along the south shore of the lake. The wind is coming from the north. You decide that you want to go back to your cottage which is on the north side of the lake. What do you do? Do you just turn your boat to the north and sail directly into the wind? You will soon find that this will not work. Your boat will stop.

What you have to do is "tack" or turn back and forth into the wind.

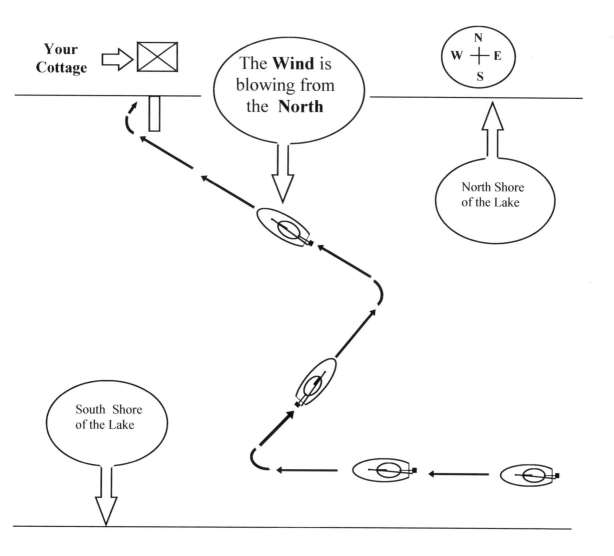

How Deep is the Water?

The Skipper must always be careful not to try to sail in water that is too shallow.

Why?

The main reason is the dagger board. The dagger board is an important part of the boat, because it helps the boat stay on a straight course, but it does stick down under water quite a way.

What if the skipper is sailing along, and not paying attention to how deep the water is? Lets say that the boat gets into very shallow water. What will happen? Oops! The dagger board is stuck in the mud or sand in the bottom of the lake, and the boat stops. That's not good. Then the skipper will have to pull up on the dagger board to free the boat.

Or worse, the dagger board might hit a rock on the bottom of the lake. This could damage the dagger board, or even the boat.

The rudder also hangs down into the water, but it is usually not such a big problem. On most small sailboats the rudder is hinged and spring loaded. That means that if the rudder hits the bottom of the lake, it "pops" backward out of the way.

The Skipper must also think about the dagger board when coming back to the beach after a sail. As the boat nears the shore, the Skipper must remember to pull up the dagger board.

Controlling your Boat

The Skipper is always in control of the sailboat.

1. Steering the Sailboat.

The Skipper controls the direction in which the boat is sailing by steering with the tiller bar, which is attached to the rudder.

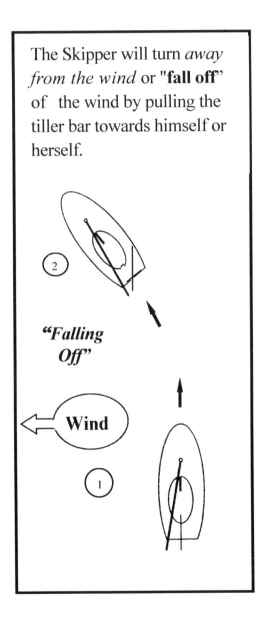

The Skipper will turn *away from the wind* or **"fall off"** of the wind by pulling the tiller bar towards himself or herself.

"*Falling Off*"

Wind

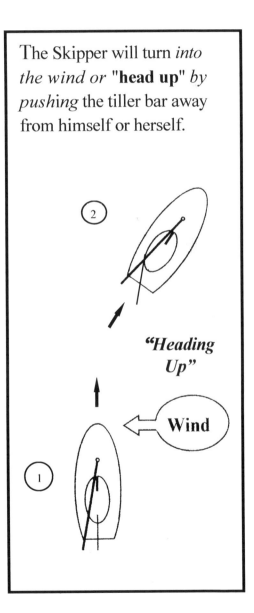

The Skipper will turn *into the wind or* **"head up"** *by pushing* the tiller bar away from himself or herself.

"*Heading Up*"

Wind

2. How fast will you go?

How fast your boat goes depends on a number of things, such as how hard the wind is blowing.

It also depends on how the skipper positions or "sets" the sail. Most of the time, unless the wind is blowing from behind the boat, the boat will go faster if the Skipper pulls on the sheet rope and brings the boom and sail over the middle of the boat.

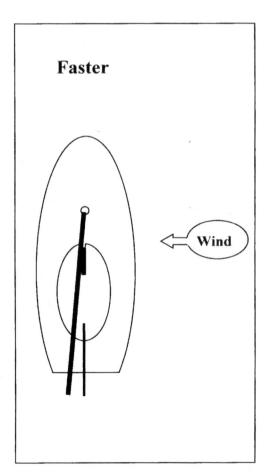

Faster

Wind

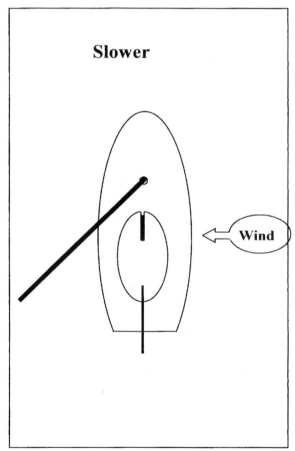

Slower

Wind

3. Don't tip over!

When your sailboat is going really fast, it will probably tip away from the wind. This tipping is called *heeling*.

If the skipper thinks that the boat is *heeling* so much that it might tip over, there are two things he or she might do to prevent a "tip over":

> 1. Let out on the sheet rope. This lets the boom (and sail) fly out to a slower position.

> 2. "Head Up" into the wind by pushing the tiller bar away.

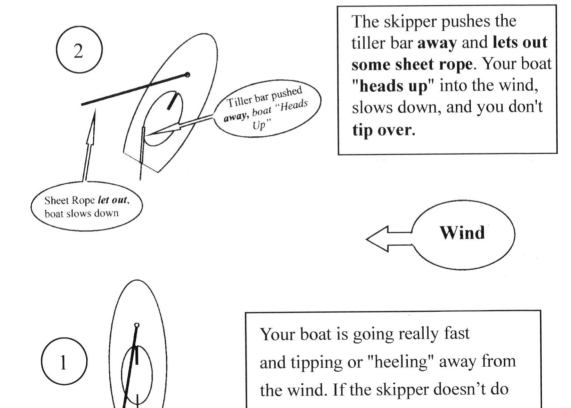

The skipper pushes the tiller bar **away** and **lets out some sheet rope**. Your boat **"heads up"** into the wind, slows down, and you don't **tip over.**

Tiller bar pushed *away, boat "Heads Up"*

Sheet Rope *let out*, boat slows down

Wind

Your boat is going really fast and tipping or "heeling" away from the wind. If the skipper doesn't do something, you may **tip over!**

4. You must learn what to do when making your boat change course.

Do you remember, earlier in this book, where you learned that you cannot sail your boat directly into the wind? Look back at page 8. To sail to your cottage on the north shore of the lake, you must turn your boat, or "change course" back and forth across the wind. This is called *tacking.*

When turning or "tacking" your boat, you will almost always turn *into* the wind. This is called *coming about.*

When the Skipper is going to come about, it is important to warn the other people on the boat so they will be ready, and not be surprised. (And so that they can keep an eye on the boom as it comes across during the turn.)

First, the Skipper, <u>using a loud </u>voice, says, **"Prepare to come about!"** Next, the Skipper says, **"Coming about".**

Just as the Skipper says this, he or she pulls in on the sheet rope to bring the boom and sail in, and, at the same time, pushes the tiller bar away.

This causes the boat to *head up* into the wind. If the Skipper keeps the tiller bar pushed away, the boat will continue to turn into the wind, until the sail and boom come across to the other side. The Skipper must now move to the other side of the boat.

Wind

3

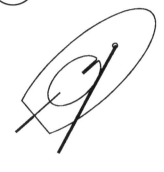

The boat keeps turning until the boom and sail go across from one side of the boat to the other side. The Skipper then moves across to the other side of the boat and sails away in a new direction.

The Skipper says "**Coming About**", pulls on the sheet rope to pull the boom and sail in, then **pushes the tiller bar away.** This causes the boat to **head up** into the wind.

2

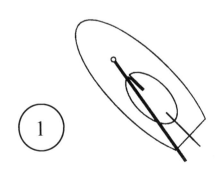

The Skipper wants to "tack". He or she says in a loud voice — **"Prepare to Come About".**

1

There is another way to turn your boat. It is called a Jibe. That word rhymes with "tribe".

A jibe should be done only by experienced sailors. It can be dangerous because, in a jibe, the boom comes from one side of the boat to the other **very fast** and could possibly bump you in the head!

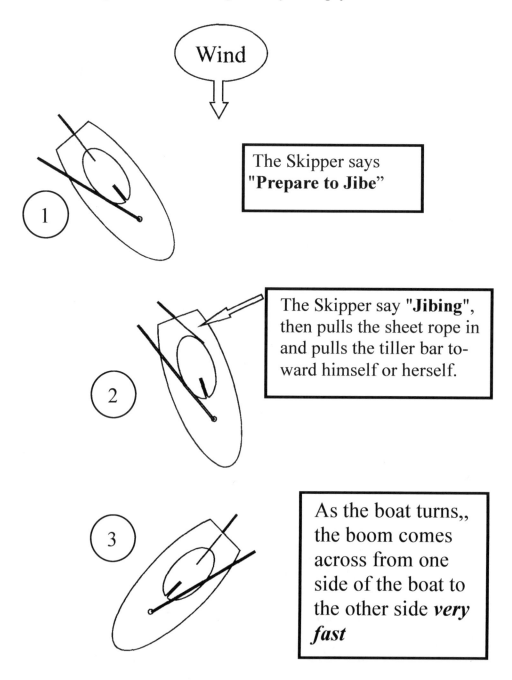

Wind

1

The Skipper says
"Prepare to Jibe"

2

The Skipper say "**Jibing**", then pulls the sheet rope in and pulls the tiller bar toward himself or herself.

3

As the boat turns,, the boom comes across from one side of the boat to the other side *very fast*

A few more Things to Know

After you have learned all of the stuff we have talked about so far, there are a few more things you will eventually want to know.

For example, there are two terms which sailors use to describe whether the wind is coming from the left (port) or from the right (starboard).

Port Tack

When the wind is blowing across the left side (the **port** side) of the boat, the boat is on a **port tack**.

Earlier in this book, we learned that the word **tack**, in sailing terms, means to *turn* the boat. Here the word **tack** has a different meaning. It just means that the wind is moving the boat while blowing across the left or **port** side of the boat.

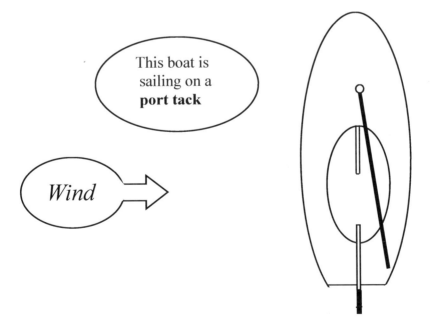

This boat is sailing on a **port tack**

Wind

Starboard Tack

When the wind is blowing across the right side (the **starboard** side) of the boat, the boat is on a **starboard tack**.

This means that the wind is moving the boat while blowing across the right or **starboard** side of the boat.

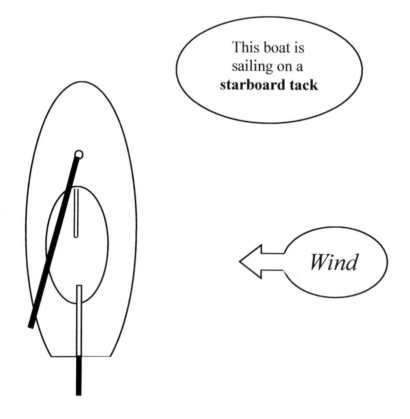

This boat is sailing on a **starboard tack**

Wind

There are also words that sailors use to describe sailing with the wind coming from different directions. These are sometimes called **"Points of Sailing"**

Wind

This boat is
**Beating into
the wind**

We learned earlier that a sailboat cannot sail *directly* into the wind. For the boat to go, the wind must be at least a little bit from the side, or from behind the boat.

Sailing with the wind coming from in front of the boat is called *beating* into the wind. *Pinching* means sailing into the wind as much as possible. When the skipper *pinches* into the wind too much, the boat will slow down or stop and the sail will flap. This flapping is called *luffing.*

When the wind is coming across the side of the boat, the boat is said to be sailing on a ***beam reach***.

Sailing on a beam reach is often a good way to make your boat go fast!

Wind

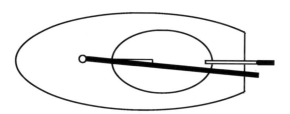

This boat is sailing on a
Beam Reach

Wind

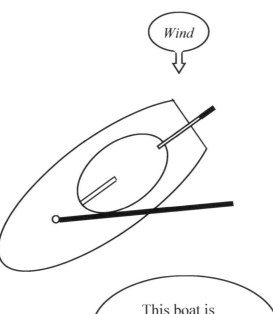

When the wind is coming across the rear (or stern) *corner* of the boat, the boat is said to be sailing on a

Broad Reach

This boat is sailing on a **Broad Reach**

Wind

When the wind is coming from behind the boat, the boat is said to be sailing on a *Run*

This boat is sailing on a **Run**

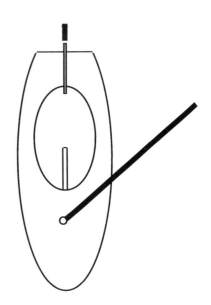

If You Do Tip Over

If your boat does tip over, don't worry. Everything will be OK, but you need to stay calm, and remember the things you have learned.

Hang onto the windward side of the boat until the mast, boom and sail are in the water, then carefully slip into the water yourself. Be careful not to get tangled in the sheet rope, and **don't ever** try to swim under the boat or under the sail.

The boat will be on it's side. Once you are in the water, work your way around to the boat to the bottom of the boat. Younger kids should wait for adult to come and help to right the boat. Older kids who have been instructed in the process of "righting" the boat (and who have been through and adult-supervised "Dump Drill"), should climb up onto the dagger board, stand up, hold onto the side of the boat, and **lean back.** Your weight will cause the boat to right itself. The mast will rise from the water.

Once the boat is upright, kick with your feet to point the front (bow) of the boat into the wind. The sail will flap (luff). Climb back onto your boat, fall off the wind, and sail away!

This Boat has tipped over. It is lying on it's side in the water. The mast, boom and sail are in the water.

This young sailor, who is wearing a life jacket, is standing on the dagger board and holding on to the side of the boat.

He will continue to hold on with his hands, and **lean back.**

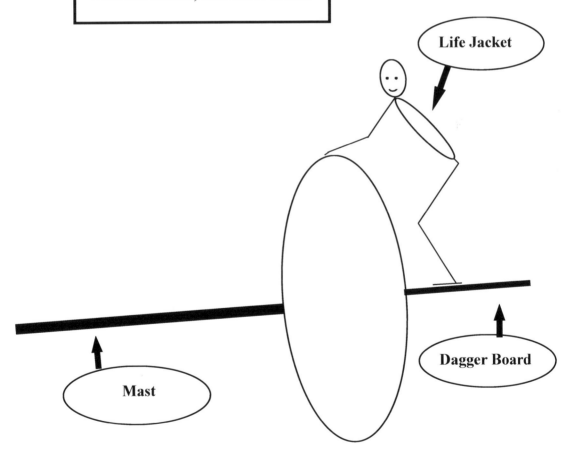

27016353R00019

Made in the USA
San Bernardino, CA
07 December 2015